# me and my piano

## repertoire *for the young pianist*

Written, selected and edited by

### Fanny Waterman

Dear Young Pianist,

The pieces in this beautifully-illustrated rainbow collection have been specially composed and arranged to help you to enjoy learning the piano. Have you ever watched a spider waltz, been to Hong Kong during rush hour, attended a huntsman's funeral, or watched a royal procession? You will find all these pieces and many more in **Me and My Piano Repertoire**.

Have fun, and practise every day!

*Fanny Waterman.*

**FABER $f\!f$ MUSIC**

# Contents

© Faber Music Ltd 1992
First published in 1992 by Faber Music Ltd,
3 Queen Square London WC1N 3AU
Music drawn by Jack Thompson
Designed and illustrated by Julia Osorno
Cover typography by Julia Osorno
Typeset by Goodfellow and Egan
Printed in England by Reflex Litho
International copyright secured
All rights reserved

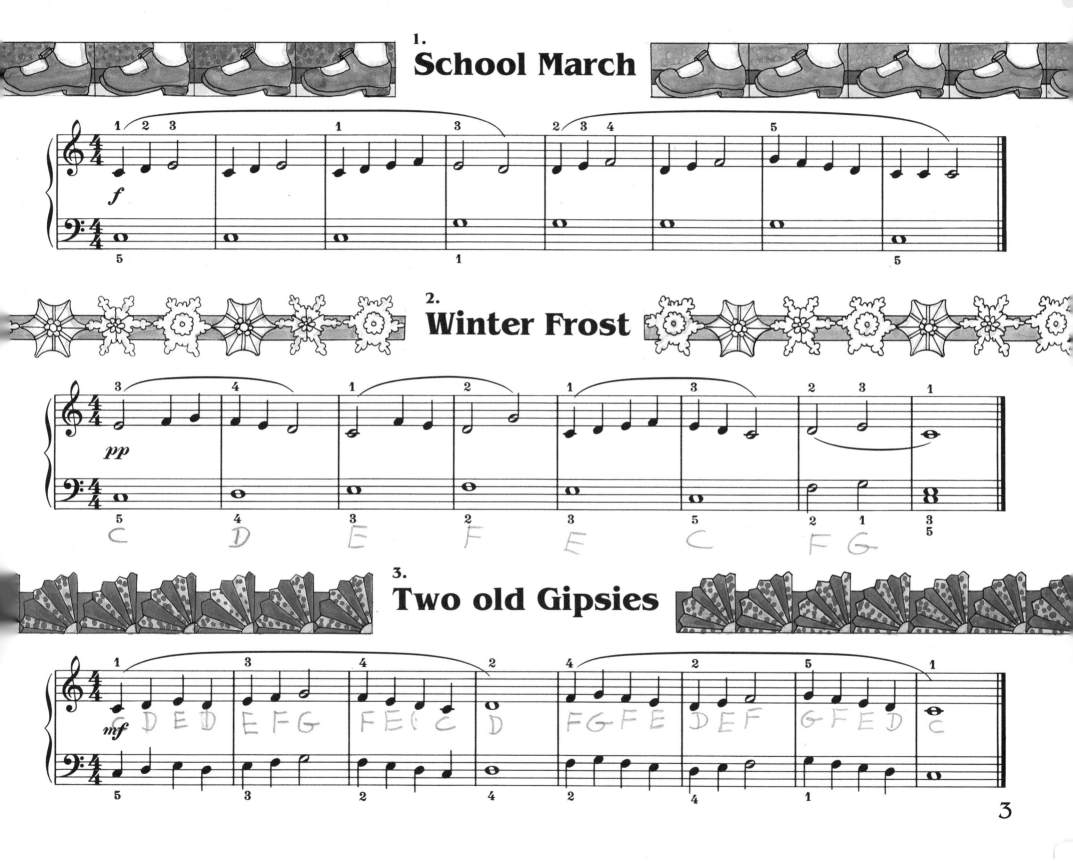

# 1. School March

# 2. Winter Frost

# 3. Two old Gipsies

**4.**
# On the Swing

**5.**
# Folk Song

6.
# Hopping Frog

7.
# Follow my Leader

5

## 8. Cossack Dance

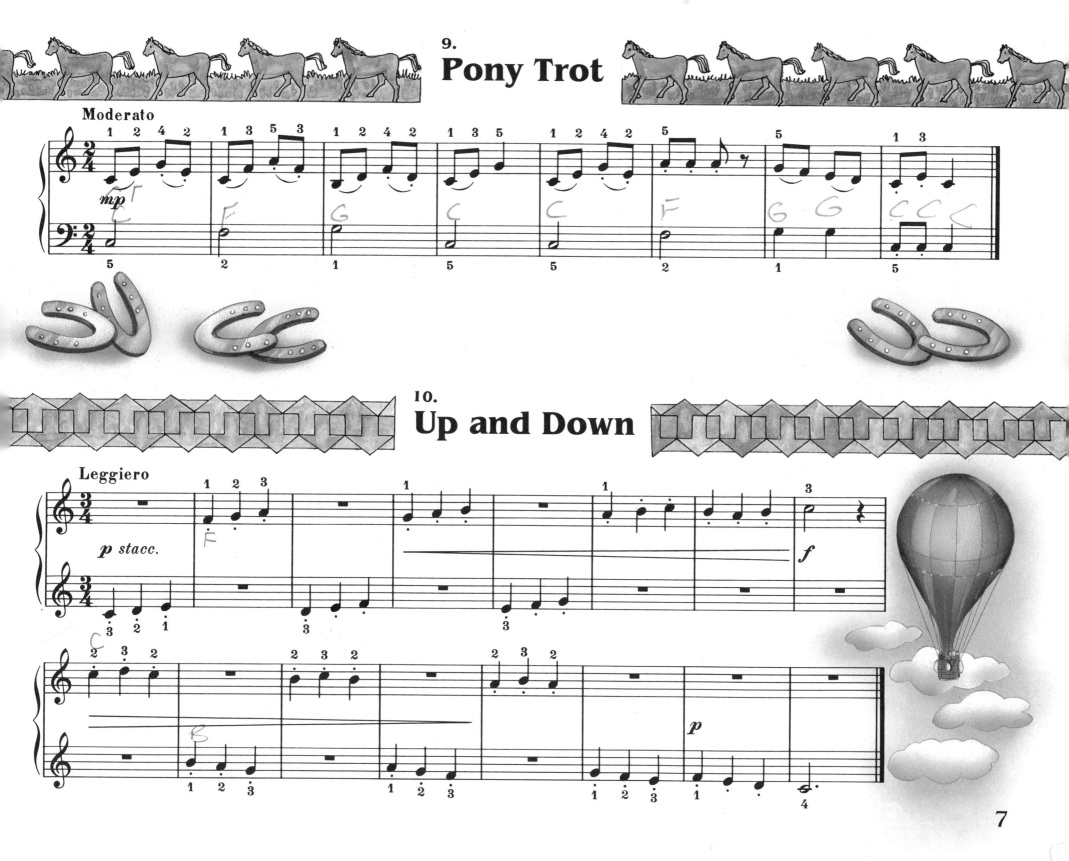

**9. Pony Trot**

**10. Up and Down**

7

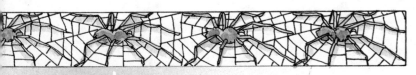

## 11.
# Spider's Waltz

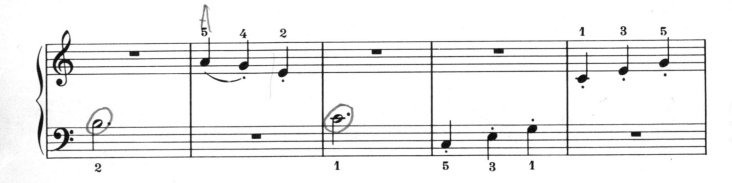

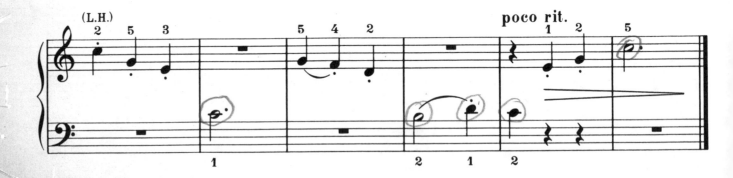

## 12.
# The Skipping Game

### 13. Moonlight

### 14. Tick Tock

## 15. Playing Together

## 16. Pop goes the Weasel

# Mountain Song

**18.**
# Sailors' Dance

Allegretto

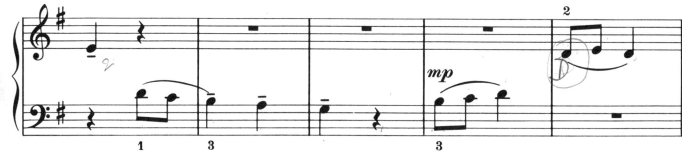

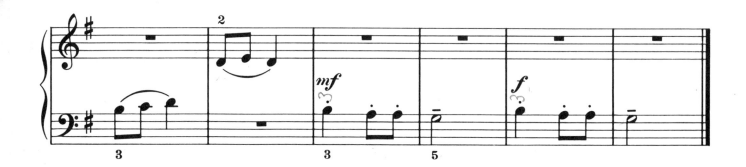

**19.**
# The Sun has got his Hat on

**20.**
# Suo-gân (*Welsh lullaby*)

14

## 21. Winter is here! (German folk song)

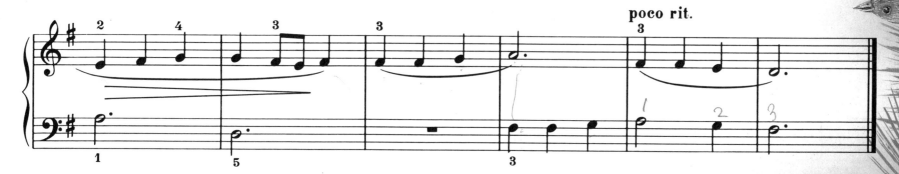

## 22. The Cello's Tune

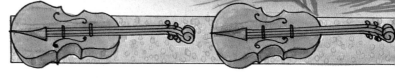

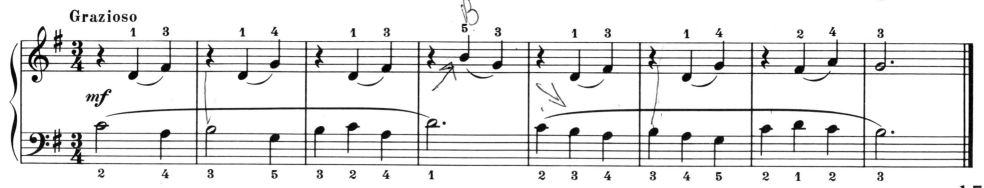

15

**23.**
# Daisy, Daisy (*duet*)

**23.**
# Daisy, Daisy (*duet*)

**PRIMO**

Grazioso

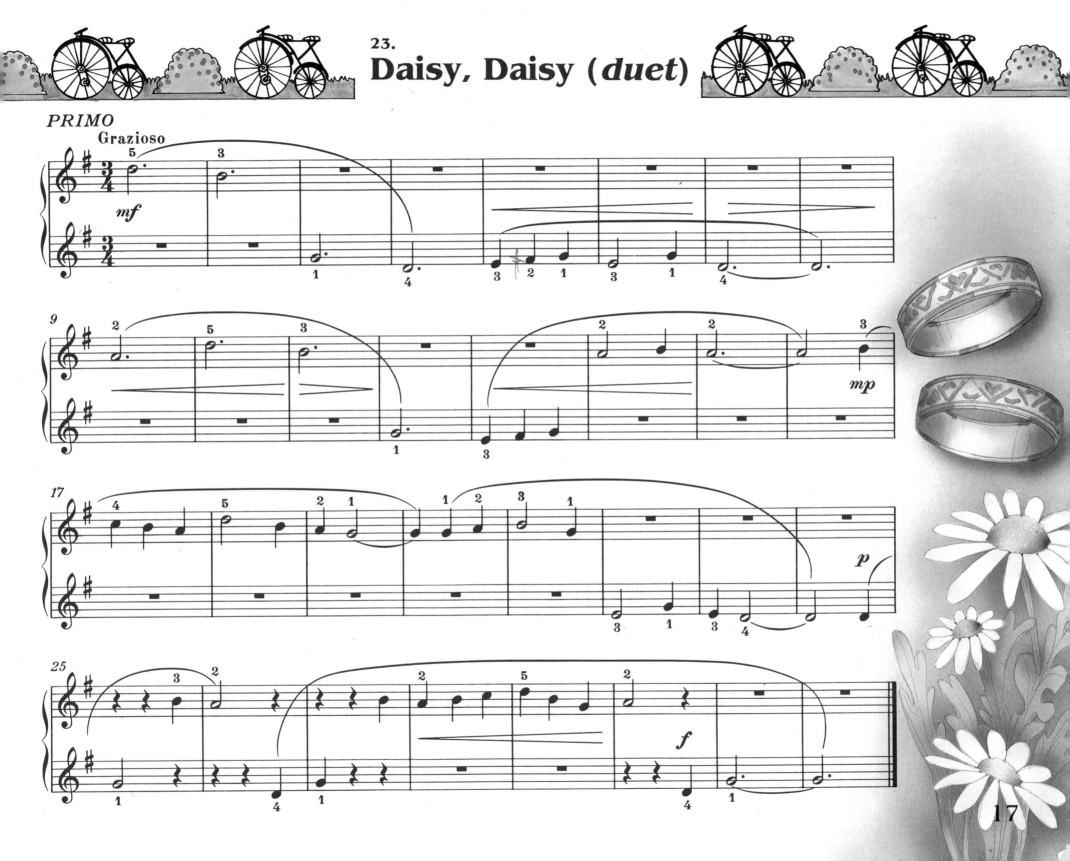

# Royal Procession

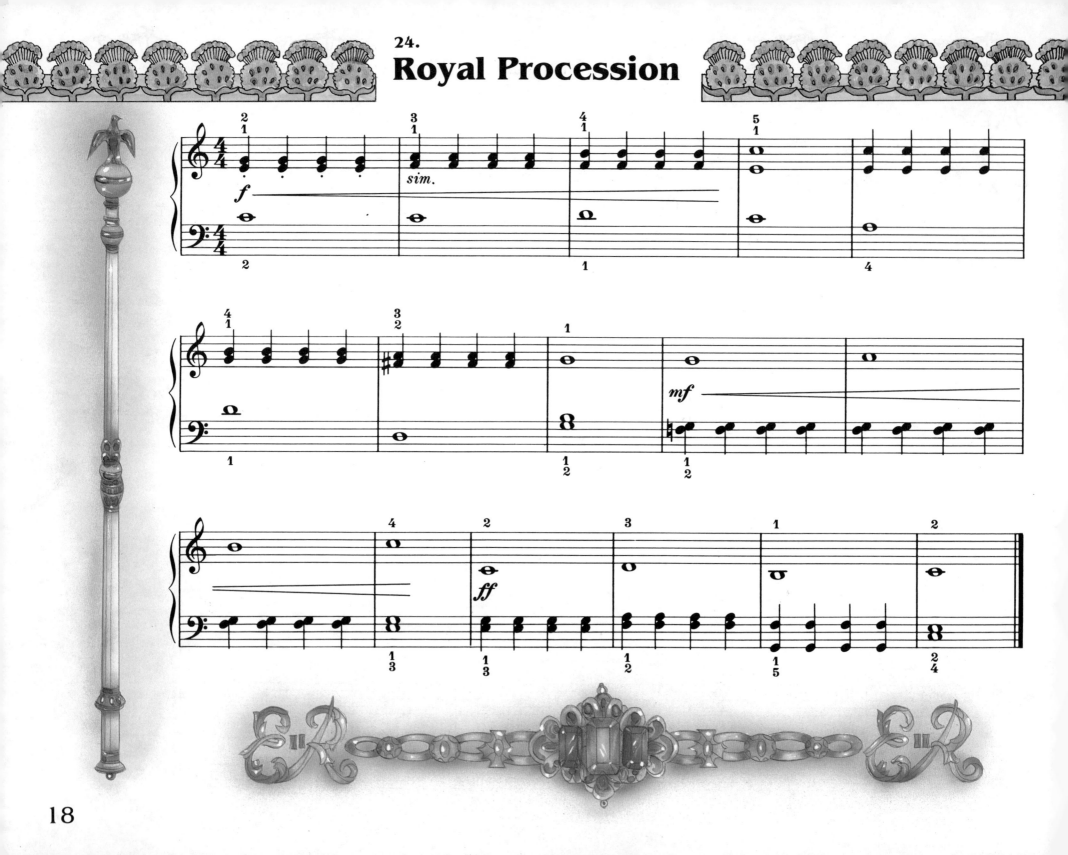

## 25.
# The Drummer Boy

Tempo di Marcia

Go on playing chords in the
left hand for as long as you want,
making a gradual *diminuendo*

### 26.
# One, Two, Three Four Five

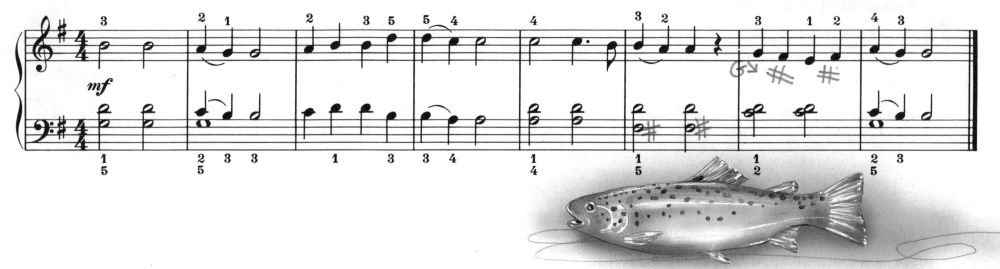

### 27.
# Be sharp!

## 28.
# Little Bo-Peep

## 29. Decorating the Christmas Tree

## 30. Hot Cross Buns

22

# The Fly and the Bumblebee

**32.**
# The Rainbow

Put both pedals down all the way through if you can reach them

**33.**

# Rush Hour in Hong Kong

Continue playing D♭ with your left hand

**34.**

# The Little Birch Tree

### 35.
# The Huntsman's Funeral

### 36.
# Study

26

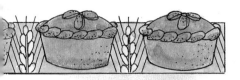

## 37.
# Dame, get up and bake your Pies

# Home, sweet Home

## 39. Early one Morning

**40.**
# Raindrops

**41.**
# Praise Him, Praise Him

**42.**
# Haktivah (*Israeli National Anthem*)

Maestoso

# 43.
# Here's a Health unto Her Majesty